P9-AOP-155

DISCARDED
Goshen Public Library

GOSHEN PUBLIC LIBRARY
601 SOUTH FIFTH STREET
GOSHEN, IN 46526-3994

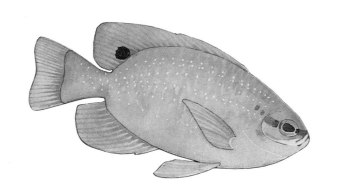

OLD SHELL, NEW SHELL

A Templar Book

Published in the United States in 2002 by The Millbrook Press, Inc.
2 Old New Milford Road, Brookfield, CT. 06804

Published simultaneously in Great Britain by Templar Publishing,
an imprint of The Templar Company plc
Pippbrook Mill, London Road, Dorking, Surrey RH4 1JE, Great Britain

Copyright © 2002 by The Templar Company plc

All rights reserved. No part of this publication may be reproduced,
stored in a retrieval system, or transmitted by any means, electronic, mechanical, photocopying,
recording, or otherwise, without the prior permission of the publishers or copyright holders.

Library 5 4 3 2 1   1 2 3 4 5 Trade

Designed by Gill McLean
Edited by A. J. Wood

Library of Congress Cataloging-in-Publication Data
Ward, Helen, 1962-
Old shell, new shell : a coral reef tale / Helen Ward.
p. cm.
"A Templar book."
Summary: A hermit crab who has outgrown his shell searches for a new one among the creatures
of Australia's Great Barrier Reef. Includes a key which identifies the coral reef animals in the
illustrations.
ISBN 0-7613-2708-8 (lib. bdg.) – ISBN 0-7613-1635-3 (trade)
1. Hermit crabs—Juvenile fiction. [1. Hermit crabs—Fiction. 2. Coral reefs and islands—Fiction.
3. Shells—Fiction. 4. Coral reef animals—Fiction. 5. Great Barrier Reef (Qld.)—Fiction. 6. Australia—
Fiction.] I. Title.
PZ10.3. W213 Ol 2002

[E]—dc21   2001045011

Printed in China

A CORAL REEF TALE
Old Shell, New Shell

by HELEN WARD

DISCARDED
Goshen Public Library

GOSHEN PUBLIC LIBRARY
601 SOUTH FIFTH STREET
GOSHEN, IN 46526-3994

The Millbook Press **M** Brookfield, Connecticut

In the watery gardens,
where sea anemones flowered
and fish as bright
as butterflies
sailed among the coral,
there lived a...

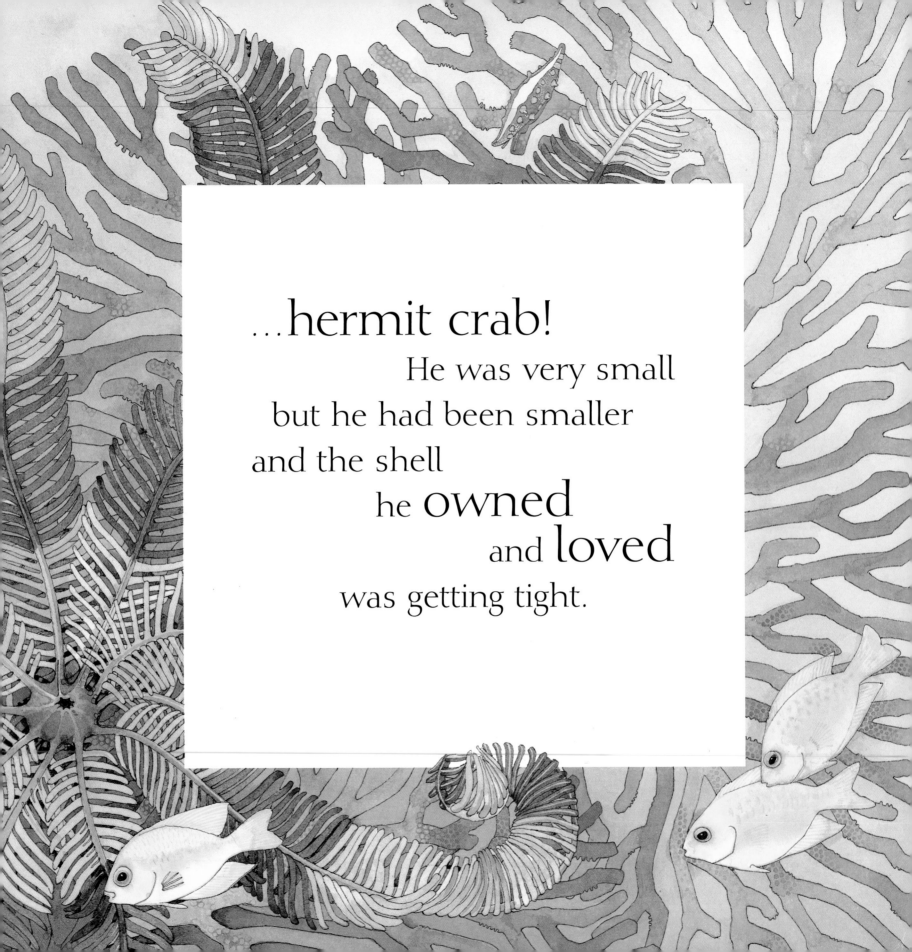

…hermit crab!
He was very small
but he had been smaller
and the shell
he owned
and loved
was getting tight.

He was very fond of his old shell.
He wanted a new one
just like it —
only larger.

"I need
a shell of this color,"
he said to a line
of passing puffer fish.
But they had not seen
a shell that color
and in any case
they were busy.

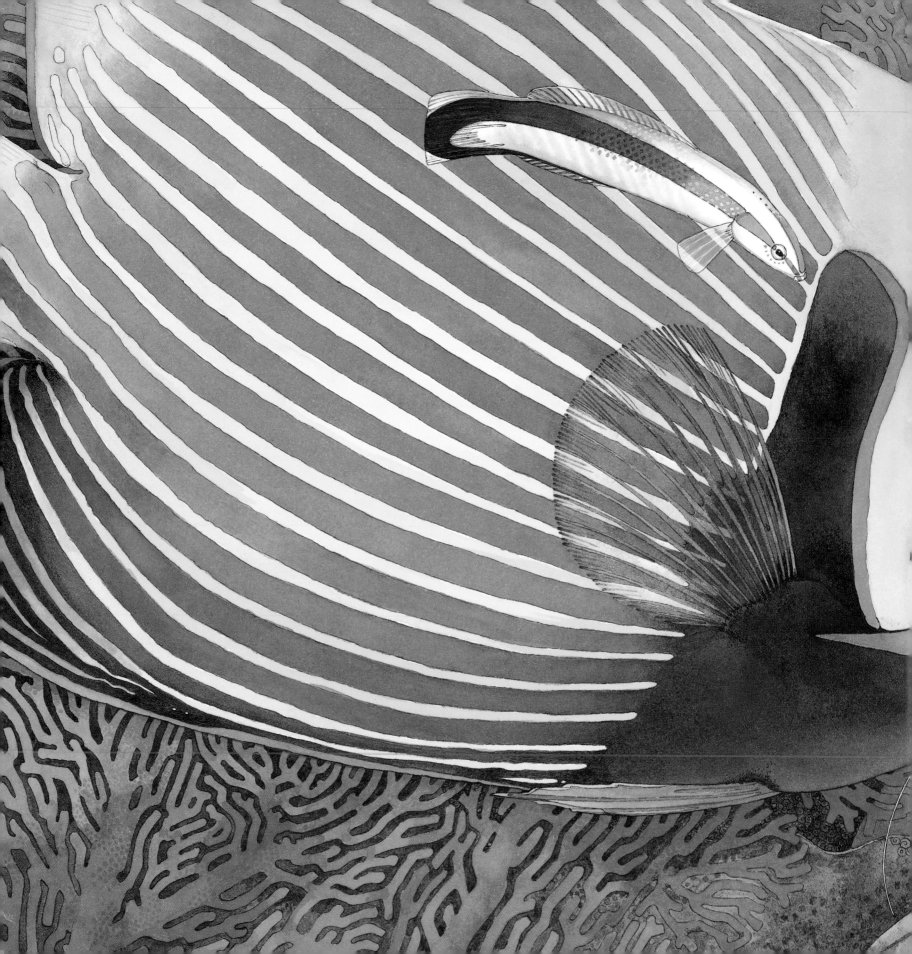

"With some of these," he said to an angelfish who really couldn't be bothered.

"And one of those," he said to a clownfish who had not seen a shell with one of those for years.

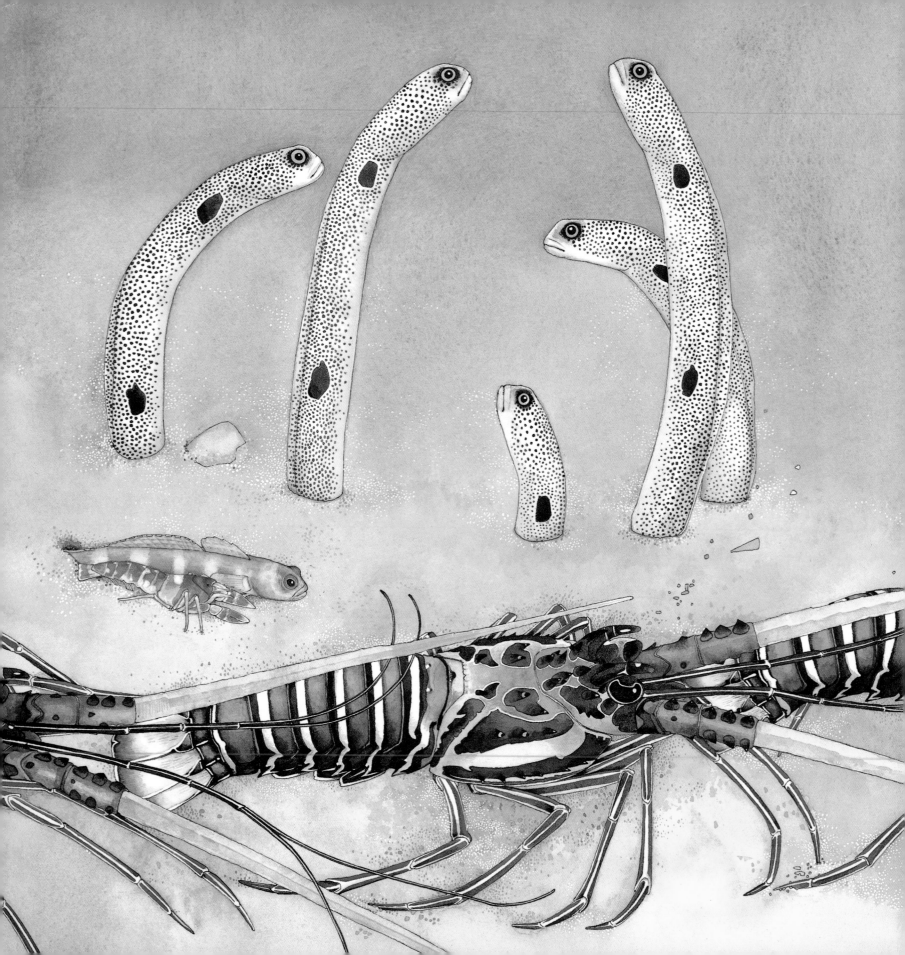

"Sort of like **this** shell," he said to a passing line of spiny lobsters,

"but **bigger!**"

Suddenly
the seabed turned
upside
down
and **knocked**
the hermit crab
clean out of
his shell.

He tumbled **down** into a shell that was much too **big**, too dull, too heavy, and too dark.

He did not want
to be eaten. So he crept
into the back of it
to be miserable

and went to sleep…

He was awakened
by being squashed.
Something else was trying
to get **inside** the big shell,
so he gave the intruder
a nip.

The Key to the Reef

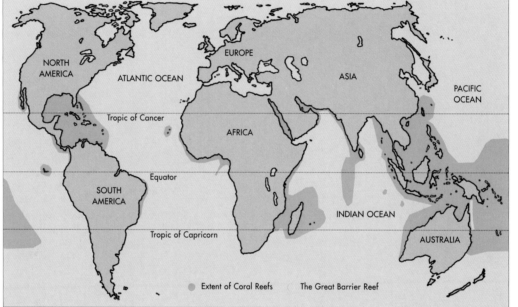

The hermit crab in this book lives on a coral reef – the Great Barrier Reef (GBR) that lies just off the coast of Australia. There are many coral reefs in the world – you can see the areas in which they occur on the map – but the GBR is one of the largest. It stretches for 1,430 miles (2,300 kilometers) along the coast of Queensland and stretches to 168 miles (270 kilometers) at its widest point. It is home to tens of thousands of different species of creatures.

All coral reefs owe their existence to colonies of millions of tiny creatures called coral polyps, which are similar to sea anemones. Polyps have soft, sac-like bodies around a bony skeleton and usually live in great communities. When the polyps die, they leave behind their hard skeletons. Other polyps grow on top of the old ones, and over the years a reef is formed.

If you went out into a garden, you might expect to see a few animals – squirrels and birds hiding in tree branches, snails under stones, insects hovering over flowers – but on the reef you would be surrounded by literally thousands of living things. An estimated 5,000 to 6,000 species of fish alone live there. Purple dottybacks, clown triggerfish, blennies, groupers, and long-nosed filefish drift in brilliantly colored shoals through the coral gardens, while countless other marine animals hide amongst the rocks. Blue starfish crawl over pink sponges, sea anemones wave their tentacles like strange flowers in the watery breeze, while in the depths of the reef a goggly-eyed octopus or fierce moray eel might be hiding in a coral cave.

The brilliant colors and striking patterns of these reef creatures often serve a vital purpose in ensuring their survival. For some, their appearance means that they can hide effectively from predators, mimicking a rock or plant or simply blending into the background so they become almost invisible. For others, their appearance is a means of attracting a mate or frightening away an enemy. Each creature has its own interesting story to tell, like our hero, the hairy red hermit crab, who adopts an empty seashell for his protection rather than grow one of his own and every so often has to find a slightly bigger one to accommodate his growing body.

You can find out more about the many species included in this book by reading the key that follows. All the creatures included in the paintings are found on the GBR and in the Indian and Pacific Oceans that surround it. Some never stray from the reef; others range the wide oceans from the Red Sea to Eastern Africa, through India right across the world to Hawaii and the Pacific Islands. There are other coral reefs around the world, off the coasts of Africa and South and Central America, scattered in a band that girdles the Earth between the Tropics of Cancer and Capricorn, all with their similar but sometimes unique inhabitants. Unfortunately, almost everywhere coral reefs are under threat. Both pollution and over-fishing by collectors are taking their toll, and many reefs around the world are now protected in an attempt to preserve them and their creatures for the future. You can find out more about reefs and what you can do to ensure their survival at the back of the book.

In the watery gardens...

In this little coral grotto the sunlight filters through the shallow water, revealing a colorful undersea "garden". Bright flowers seem to grow from the rocks, but look closer and you'll see that the plants in this garden are in fact tiny creatures – sea slugs with their strange shapes and vivid colors, sea worms and anemones with tentacles as brightly colored as any petal, and the frills and spikes of countless types of coral, each one a collection of tiny polyps. Brighter still are the coral-loving fish, flitting brilliantly back and forth like underwater butterflies with their gaudy patterns and glistening scales – all part of a coral carnival under the sea!

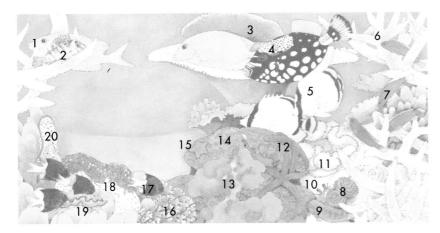

1. Coral rabbitfish (*Siganus corallinus*)
Despite their pretty colors, these fish have venomous spines within their fins that can inflict a nasty wound. They like to live among the rocks in warm shallow waters.

2. Dwarf hawkfish (*Cirrhitichthys falco*)
At 2.4 inches (6 centimeters) this is one of the smallest hawkfish on the reef. Its blotchy colors camouflage it among the reef rocks.

3 and 6. Staghorn coral (*Acropora hyacinthus* and *A. formosa*)
Coral comes in all sorts of shapes and colors. Different polyps grow together to form the varied shapes that give corals their common names. Staghorn coral has antler-like branches or plates that provide shelter for many types of fish.

4. Clown triggerfish (*Balistoides conspicillum*)
Triggerfish get their name from a long spine – part of their dorsal fin – that most of the time lies flat along their back. When threatened, they can flick the spine up for protection or use it to wedge themselves into a rocky crevice.

5. Vagabond butterflyfish (*Chaetodon vagabundus*)
So called because their bright colors and patterns often resemble the wings of butterflies, these fish have delicately pointed snouts for exploring the coral crannies in search of food.

7. Purple dottyback (*Pseudochromis porphyreus*)
Like the colors of many other reef fish, the brilliant purple of the dottyback comes from tiny pigment cells in the fish's skin. Many fish can expand and contract these cells to change their color, to match either their background or their mood!

8. Christmas tree worm (*Spirobranchus giganteus*)
One of the fan worms, this creature is named after the plume-like tentacles through which it breathes and feeds.

9. Bicolor blenny (*Ecsenius bicolor*)
Blennies lay their eggs in crevices on the reef, sometimes in abandoned shells or worm tubes. The male guards them until they hatch.

10. Hairy red hermit crab (*Dardanus megistos*)
Did you spot our hero peeping out from his hideaway? You can find out more about hermit crabs below.

11. Soft coral (*Sarcophyton*)
These corals often form mushroom, funnel, or cup shapes and can grow to more than 20 inches (0.5 meter) across.

12. Blue starfish (*Linckia laevigata*)
Like other starfish, the blue variety uses its five arms to pry open the shellfish that form the main part of its diet. If it loses an arm, it simply grows another in its place!

13. Tree coral (*Dendronephthya*)
With their branches and spiny clusters of polyps, these corals look like strange underwater trees. Many small creatures find hiding places within this type of coral, and the prickly surface gives them added protection from their enemies.

14. Brain coral (*Favites*)
This coral forms great brain-like, lumpy clumps with curious ridges all over the surface.

15. Queensland starfish (*Tosia queenslandensis*)
This tiny sea star grows to only 1.2 inches (3 centimeters) across. It is found only on coral reefs around Australia.

16. Fire coral (*Millepora*)
Also known as stinging coral, the polyps of this species have stinging tentacles that are painful to humans.

17. Bicolor chromis (*Chromis margaritifer*)
These common fish are often seen swimming in groups, called shoals, over the coral beds.

18. Sea anemone (*Heterodactyla hemprichii*)
Sea anemones look like strange flowers anchored to the reef rocks. They use their inward-folding tentacles to pass food toward their central mouth and, if frightened, withdraw them so they are left looking just like a blob of jelly.

19 and 20. Sea slugs (*Chromodoris coi* and *C. kuniei*)
Distantly related to land-dwelling slugs and snails, sea slugs come in a fantastic variety of shapes, colors, and patterns. They live mainly on tiny creatures such as hydroids and sponges.

...hermit crab!

There are many different types of hermit crabs. They belong to the same group of animals as shrimps, lobsters, crayfish, and true crabs, and also the land-loving woodlice and pill bugs. All hermit crabs have one thing in common. Unlike most crabs, which grow a shell to protect their soft bodies, hermit crabs simply find empty seashells to live in instead. As they grow, hermit crabs discard their old adopted shells, finding bigger ones to accommodate their growing bulk. Some crabs seem to have a liking for particular kinds of shells, but one thing is for certain: when it's time to move house, our hero must be quick – the longer he is outside a shell with no protection, the more likely it is that he'll be snapped up by a hungry fish!

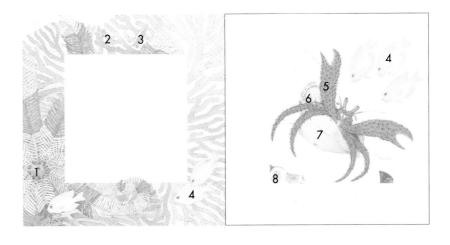

1. Crinoid featherstar (*Petasometra clarae*)
They may look like strange plants, but featherstars are a type of animal. Although they can use their long arms to swim, these creatures very rarely move, spending most of their lives anchored to the reef where they filter seawater for microscopic particles of food.

2. Gorgonian sea fan (*Gorgonia sp.*)
A type of coral, sea fans can grow to many yards in height. Like all corals, they need light to survive, so you will not find them in water beyond the reach of sunlight. Sea fans grow in many different shapes, covering the reef like colorful shrubbery.

3. Spindle cowrie (*Phenacovolva angasi*)
There are two main types of seashell – gastropods, which have one solid shell, and bivalves, which have two parts to their shell, hinged to open and shut like a case. The spindle cowrie is a gastropod, drawing its fleshy body inside its shell when threatened. It is often found living amongst the branches of sea fans. In some parts of the world, cowries were once used instead of money!

4. Lemon damselfish (*Pomacentrus muluccensis*)
Damsels are easy to spot on almost any reef, swimming in large shoals through the sunlit waters. Like many reef fish, they have brush-like teeth with which they eat the minute plants and animals that live among the coral.

5. Hairy red hermit crab (*Dardanus megistos*)
This hermit crab has found the shell of a bat volute (*Cymbiola vespertilio*) to use as its portable home. The crab's claws are shaped in such a way that when it withdraws into its shell they fit together to form an almost unbreakable armored door across the entrance hole. The claws are also useful in breaking open the shells of mollusks whose soft bodies the crab will then eat!

6. Hermit crab anemone (*Calliactis sp.*)
Some kinds of sea anemone are commonly found attached to the shells of hermit crabs. The crab and the anemone form what is known as a symbiotic relationship, where each gains something from the other. In this case, the anemone is moved around to new feeding grounds on the crab's back and also picks up particles of food that drift free of whatever its host is eating, and the crab gains camouflage and some protection from the anemone, which has a tiny sting in each of its many tentacles.

7. Bat volute (*Cymbiola vespertilio*)
There are over sixty different types of volute found in the waters around Australia. Their graceful shapes and beautiful colors make them popular with collectors. When alive, they burrow in the sand of shallow seas, catching and eating other small sea creatures.

8. Sea squirt (*Aplidium protectans*)
Sea squirts are built rather like plastic bags. They take in water through one opening on their body, filter it for food particles, and then squirt it out of another hole. They'll also squirt water if disturbed in the hope that it will frighten away any predator.

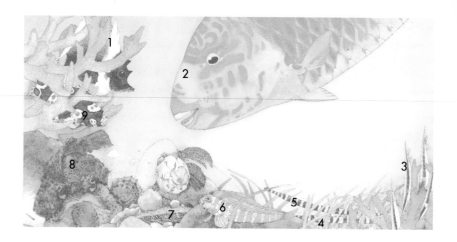

3. Razorfish (*Aeoliscus strigatus*)
These fish, which are as thin as a wafer, have the clever habit of swimming vertically in groups, twisting and turning to look just like waving grass.

4. Seagrass (*Cymodocea serrulata*)
Seagrass often forms great underwater meadows around coral reefs. Although only a few animals (such as turtles, sea urchins, and some mollusks) eat the grass itself, many feed on the algae that cover its surface.

5. Ringed pipefish (*Doryrhamphus dactylophorus*)
The pipefish's stripes help to hide it from its enemies among the weeds in which it lives.

6. Banded blenny (*Salarias fasciatus*)
The banded blenny's markings are not the only thing that helps this fish to hide from its enemies. If danger threatens, it will flatten itself against the seabed, remaining motionless and very hard to spot.

7. Pen shell (*Atrina pectinata*)
Wedged into its rocky crevice, the plain brown shell of this bivalve conceals the brilliantly striped body of the creature that lives inside. These shellfish spend their lives embedded in sand or rocks with only the top of their shell visible. They open the shell and extend part of their soft body, known as a mantle, out to filter the water for food.

8. Estuary stonefish (*Synanceia horrida*)
A master of disguise, the stonefish uses its clever camouflage to help it catch unsuspecting prey rather than for protection. Its blotchy brown scales conceal many venom-laden spines that can inflict a deadly wound.

9. Many-spotted sweetlips (*Plectorhinchus chaetodontoides*)
Like some other reef fish, this species changes color as it grows. When young, its brown and white spots help to hide it from predators.

He was very fond...

The hermit crab uses its shell when it needs to hide away from danger. Other creatures do not have the same protection and rely on clever coloring and shape to keep them hidden on the reef.

1. Humphead bannerfish (*Heniochus varius*)
With its curiously shaped fins and markings, this fish becomes hard to distinguish from the spiky coral in which it lives.

2. Blue-barred parrotfish (*Scarus gnobban*)
With its colorful scales, the parrotfish makes no attempt to hide, relying on its size and bulk to deter predators. Some species grow as big as 40 inches (100 centimeters), and most are as bright as the birds after which they are named. All parrotfish have strong beak-like mouths and special grinding teeth that they use to break off lumps of coral in search of food.

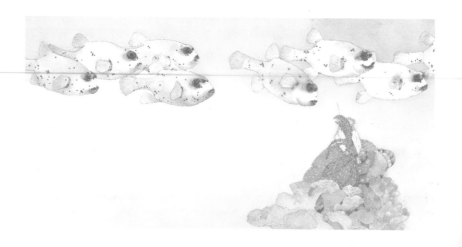

I need a shell...

The black spotted puffer fish (*Arothron nigropunctatus*) is one of a whole group of fish that have developed a rather ingenious way of protecting themselves from danger. Rather than relying on camouflage or venomous spines, these fish can gulp water so rapidly that their bodies swell up into little balls many times the size of the fish that seconds before may have looked like a tasty morsel. The only problem is that, once inflated, the puffer fish cannot move very well. It has to wait several minutes before it can expel all the water and swim away!

With some of these...

The reef is full of strange partnerships between creatures in which each side benefits in some way from living with or near the other. These symbiotic relationships ensure the continued survival of some species and improve the health of others.

1. Cleaner wrasse (*Labroides dimidiatus*)
This underwater cleaner performs a very important job for much larger fish such as the emperor angelfish shown in the same picture, picking parasites and other unwanted rubbish from its scales. Even though the cleaner wrasse could easily be eaten by its host, the regular cleaning service it offers is much more valuable than a quick mouthful of food, and big fish will not only stay still in order to be cleaned but will even stop breathing while their gill linings are cleaned. The cleaner wrasse benefits too – a free lunch is the reward for such effort!

2. Emperor angelfish (*Pomacanthus imperator*)
Also known as the imperial angelfish, this fish is one of the most striking on the reef. It has a dark mask around its eyes and a body covered in yellow stripes, which are thought to lead any predator's eye away from its delicate head area. Young angelfish are more camouflaged with their covering of blue and white stripes. Adults can often be seen lining up for a wash and brush-up from the cleaner wrasse.

3. Acorn barnacle (*Tetraclita sp.*)
Although they look very like shellfish, barnacles are much more closely related to crabs and shrimps. They begin life as larvae, spending their time swimming through the sea until they change into their adult form and attach themselves like small volcanoes to rocks, shells, dead coral, or even the surface of passing whales or turtles, where they spend the rest of their lives. To feed, the barnacle thrusts out tiny leg-like appendages called cirri between the hard plates of its shell. These cirri are covered in fine bristles that pick up microscopic bits of food when they are wafted through the seawater. There are over 800 different types of barnacles some of which have fleshy stalks beneath their shells.

And one of those...

Like the cleaner wrasse and the emperor angelfish, the clownfish and the anemone both gain something from the other – the fish gains protection from its enemies among the anemone's stinging tentacles while the anemone gets the leftovers from the fish's lunch!

1. Cleaner shrimp (*Lysmata amboinensis*)
Like cleaner fish, cleaner shrimps perform a vital service for many reef fish. They often occupy permanent "stations" on the reef that are regularly visited by their customers, who signal for the shrimps to climb aboard their scales to eat up tiny parasites.

2. Longnose filefish (*Oxymonacanthus longirostris*)
Filefish, so called because their scales are covered with small spines that give their bodies a prickly texture, have a long snout specially developed to probe the coral polyps for food. Their bright colors attract mates during the breeding season. The males also perform territorial displays, dancing through the water, flicking their tails to warn off rivals and win the attention of any watching lady fish!

3. Polkadot grouper (*Cromileptes altivelis*)
Also known as the barramundi or humpbacked rock cod, this fish belongs to a group that includes some of the reef's largest fish. The Queensland grouper can grow to over 9 feet (270 centimeters) and reach a weight of over 882 pounds (400 kilograms). Groupers can also change sex as they grow, turning from females into males.

4. Magnificent sea anemone (*Heteractis magnifica*)
The anemone uses its stinging tentacles to stun its prey of tiny fish and other small sea creatures, but does not seem to mind harboring the little clownfish in return for sharing in its meals. The anemone will pick up and ingest any tiny particles that are carried away in the water from whatever its fishy friends have caught. Some anemones of this kind can grow to over 3 feet (over 1 meter) in width and can live for over a hundred years once established.

5. Clown anemonefish (*Amphiprion percula*)
Unlike other small reef fish, clownfish are immune to the anemone's sting thanks to a special mucus that coats their scales. Instead they get some protection from their enemies by living among these stinging "flowers," and in return any food particles they drop get passed on to their host. There are several different types of anemonefish. Each type is generally associated with a particular type of sea anemone and several fish may live together on one "host." The clown anemonefish is usually found living among *Heteractis* anemones and grows to 4 inches (10 centimeters) long.

6. Blue-ringed angelfish (*Pomacanthus annularis*)
One of the larger angelfish, this species can grow to 12 inches (30 centimeters). If agitated, these fish produce a loud drumming noise by vibrating an organ inside their bodies known as a swim bladder.

Sort of like this...

Unlike the hermit crab, most other marine crustaceans have hard outer bodies to protect them. The spiny lobster is covered in a hard, jointed armor that is impervious to all but the strongest teeth. It is no match for a man-made net or basket though, and many of these creatures are caught and eaten by humans.

1. Garden eel (*Heteroconger hassi*)
These strange sea creatures get their name from their habit of congregating in groups, half submerged in the sand of the seabed. Only the top half of their bodies can be seen, swaying back and forth like some kind of peculiar plant.

2. Goby shrimp (*Alphius randalli*) and 3. Banded shrimp goby (*Amblyelestris fasciata*)
In another curious undersea partnership, the goby shrimp provides a burrow for the goby fish, constantly keeping it clean and tidy. The fish returns the favor by guarding the entrance, flicking its tiny tail to signal to its partner when it is safe to emerge.

4. Purple spiny lobster (*Panulirus versicolor*)
Also known as the painted crayfish or rock lobster, this curious-looking creature hides in crevices during the day, coming out at night to feed.

5.Blue damselfish (*Pomacentrus pavo*)
These fish swim in shimmering shoals, hovering above the coral in their search for food. As with most fish, their bright colors disappear within minutes when they die.

Suddenly the seabed turned upside down...

Another master of disguise, the flounder, is responsible for turning our hero's world upside down. Like many other flat fish, the flounder spends most of its life lying on the sea floor, partly covered by sand. It is hard to spot until it suddenly flaps its fins and swims away.

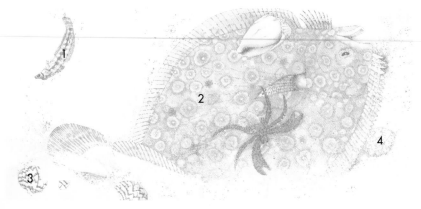

1. Sharpnose sandperch (*Parapercis cylindrica*)
Another fish of the seabed, the sandperch is small but has a mouth full of sharp, pointed teeth.

2. Panther flounder (*Bothus pantherinus*)
The color of this flounder varies to match the sea floor where it spends much of its time. Over millions of years of evolution, it has adapted so well to this low-lying life that both its eyes have moved to face upwards on the top of its head!

3. Hieroglyphic venus clam (*Lioconcha hieroglyphica*) and 4. Chocolate-flamed venus clam (*L. castrensis*)
With their beautifully patterned shells, it seems a shame that these shellfish spend most of their lives submerged in the sand and mud of the seabed.

He tumbled down...

Vast numbers of different creatures inhabit coral reefs, making them second only to rain forests in richness of species. But not all are obvious to the eye. Scientists believe there may be thousands more creatures waiting to be discovered, tiny invertebrates that live within the cracks and crevices of the reef itself.

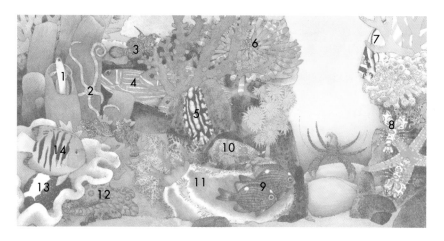

1. Elegant firefish (*Nemateleotris decora*)
This pretty little fish will often take refuge inside sea sponges such as this purple *Halidona*.

2. Brittlestar (*Ophiarachnella gorgonia*)
Brittlestars are the most active of the starfishes and can move with considerable speed on their long arms.

3. Mandarinfish (*Synchiropus splendidus*)
The brilliant colors of the mandarinfish may make it look obvious, but it is one of the world's greatest mimics – like an underwater chameleon, it can change color to become almost invisible to its predators.

4. Crown squirrelfish (*Sargocentron diadema*)
The squirrelfish, like its namesake, hides away in nooks and crannies, emerging to feed on crustaceans. It can make all sorts of curious noises by vibrating an organ within its body called a swim bladder. No one knows quite what the noises are for, but scientists believe they may be used to entice a mate or frighten away a rival.

5. Sea slug (*Phyllidia varicola*)
As with many sea slugs, the bright colors and pattern of this species are a warning of its horrible taste.

6. Slate pencil sea urchin (*Heterocentrotus mammillatus*)
This sea urchin can move about the reef using its spines. They are attached to its body with ball-and-socket joints that allow the spines to move in any direction.

7. Ornate butterflyfish (*Chaetodon ornatus*)
The seemingly random stripes on this butterflyfish help to hide its head, masking its eye area from attack by predators.
8. Orchid shrimp (*Hymenocera picta*)
Also known as the harlequin or painted shrimp, this crustacean may be easily seen in isolation, but its bold markings break up its outline so effectively that, when among the coral, it can be hard to spot. It feeds on starfish.
9. Three-spot dascyllus (*Dascyllus trimaculatus*)
These fish often live among sea anemones when young, moving away as adults to swim amongst the coral.
10. Textile cone (*Conus textile*)
Don't be fooled by the beauty of this mollusk. It has a venomous, harpoon-like tooth which can kill a human.
11. Sea cucumber (*Pseudocolchirus violaceus*)
Despite being named after a vegetable, the sea cucumber is an animal. It gets its name from its widespread use in Asia as a base for soups!
12. Blue-ringed octopus (*Hapalochlaena maculosa*)
Although tiny compared to its giant relatives, at almost 3 inches (7 centimeters) this cephalopod can produce an extremely powerful venom.
13. Egg cowrie (*Ovula ovum*)
Despite its name, this glossy white seashell is not a true cowrie but a close relative. It can extend part of its fleshy body, called the mantle, out and over its shell to help hide it among the coral.
14. Flame angelfish (*Centropyge loriculus*)
This colourful angelfish feeds on sponges and small invertebrates.

He did not want to be eaten...

At the very bottom of the reef, where the sunlight barely filters through the water, a different set of creatures can be found. Fierce predators lurk in the shadows, so it is just as well that our hermit crab has found another volute shell to hide in – even one that is too big – for remaining uncovered for long could be fatal...

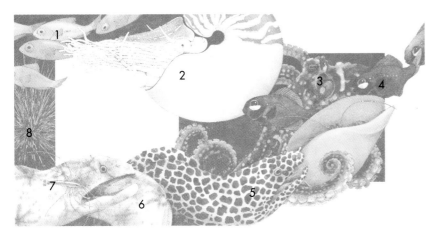

1. Golden sweeper (*Parapriacanthus ransonneti*)
Its large eyes are a clue to this fish's gloomy habitat – it spends its life swimming in schools in caves and other areas with little light.
2. Nautilus (*Nautilus pompilius pompilius*)
This strange creature may look like a giant seashell, but its nearest living relatives are the octopuses and squids. Fossil remains show that nautiloids have existed in the world's oceans for over 500 million years, swimming majestically through the tropical waters. The nautilus can adjust its buoyancy by filling or emptying gas-filled chambers within its shell, enabling it to float at whatever level it wishes.

3. Common reef octopus (*Octopus cyenea*)
The octopus is probably the most intelligent invertebrate (creature without a backbone), since it has a brain capable of learning. The largest species has tentacles that can spread almost 12 feet (3.7 meters)!
4. Small flashlight fish (*Photoblepharon palpebratus*)
Special light-producing bacteria live in the organs beneath each eye of this fish. They produce a weak light that helps the fish to see in its gloomy surroundings, but are also used as a lure to attract prey and communicate with others of its kind.
5. Black-spotted moray (*Gymnothorax tessellata*)
Like many moray eels, this splendidly spotty creature lives a retiring life lurking among the rocks. It has a vicious bite and can grow to 80 inches (203 centimeters) long.
6. Starry moray (*Echidna nebulosa*)
A fierce predator that preys on fish and other small reef creatures, this eel would soon gobble up a hermit crab unwise enough to leave its shell.
7. Humpback cleaner shrimp (*Lysmata sp.*)
This cleaner shrimp is not afraid of the moray, depite its needle-sharp teeth, and will even clean inside its mouth!
8. Diadem sea urchin (*Diadema setosum*)
The delicate spines of this sea urchin are sharp and venomous, but they do not prevent its becoming food for some fish such as triggerfish and puffers.

He was awakened...

1. Sea slug (*Chromodoris lubocki*)
Like their garden-dwelling relatives, sea slugs can move swiftly over the rocks.
2. Blue puller fish (*Chromis caerulea*)
The color of this fish varies from blue to green and, thanks to the construction of the pigment cells within its scales, the color seems to shimmer in the sunlit water.
3. Comet (*Caloplesiops altivelis*)
This wonderful mimic hides with its head in a crevice, leaving only its tail showing. The large eye spot on its side makes it look like the head of a fierce moray eel poking out of the rock – sure to keep its enemies at bay!
4. Purple hermit crab (*Dardanus guttatus*)
This hermit crab can easily be identified by the blue spots on its legs. It grows to over 3 inches (8 centimeters) long.
5. Nine-banded cardinalfish (*Apogon novemfasciatus*)
Cardinalfish, like other members of their family, take great care of their young. Some species even take their eggs into their mouths for safe keeping!
6. Turban shell (*Turbo sp.*)
These beautiful shells come in many colors and patterns. Their name comes from the Latin word *turbo*, meaning "spinning top."

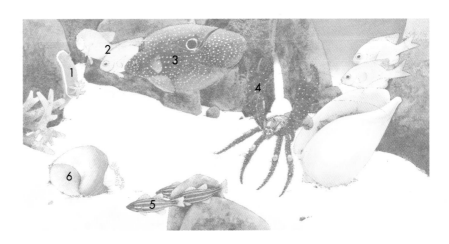

She had grown too big...

At last both hermit crabs have found new shells to fit. They will have to go through the same process several more times during their life on the reef, but for now at least each is safe in its new suit of adopted armor!

1. Spotted boxfish (*Ostracion meleagris*) Like all boxfish, this species has a box-like arrangement of bony plates around its body to protect it from predators. Scientists once thought that the fish pictured here were two separate species. They now know that the brown spotted fish is the female and the green and blue one is her mate!

2. Bicolor goatfish (*Parupeneus baberinoide*)
Named for the barbels that hang from its chin, this fish forages over the seabed using its sensitive "whiskers" to help in the hunt for food.

3. White-barred triggerfish (*Rhinecanthus aculeatus*)
In addition to the spine that lies along its back, this fish also has a patch of spines on each side of its tail. Like many triggerfish, this species looks very different when viewed head-on. It will face any attacker with its thin, triangular body and flick round to show its much larger, more dramatic side profile in the hope that its enemy will be frightened away.

4. Powder-blue surgeonfish
(*Acanthurus leucosternon*)
This fish may look harmless, but like all surgeonfish it carries a sharp spine on each side of its tail that it will use to slash an attacker.

5. Pyjama wrasse
(*Pseudocheilinus hexataenia*)
The males of this species are much more gaudily colored than their mates. Unlike some other fish, wrasse lay many eggs that float to the surface and are not cared for in any way by their parents.

6. Purple-backed dottyback (*Pseudochromis diadema*)
The brilliant colours of the dottybacks are used by the males in territorial displays during the breeding season.

7. Volute shell (*Amoria grayi*)
As with many seashells, the plain shell of this volute conceals a strikingly striped body.

8. Yellowtail poison fangblenny (*Meiacanthus atrodorsalis*)
These fish are named for their sharp, hollow teeth, which are connected to venomous glands.

9. Doubletooth soldierfish (*Myripristis hexagona*)
Also know as squirrelfish, these nocturnal fish hide under coral shelves in the daytime. They have rough scales and saucer-shaped eyes.

10. Sea slug (*Flabellina exoptata*)
The curious fleshy lobes on this sea slug's body have stinging cysts at their tips to deter predators. The slugs gain this defense mechanism by eating the stinging cells of polyps and storing them for their own use. In addition, the lobes help to camouflage the slug.

11. Colonial anemone (*Amphianthus sp.*)
Unlike some other types of anemone, the colonial anemone is often found living in groups.

12. Striped triplefin (*Helcogramma striata*)
The bright white stripes of this fish help to camouflage it among the sponges, corals, and sea fans with which it lives.

13. Giant clam (*Tridacna maxima*)
One of the largest shellfish in the world, the giant clam may grow to over 4 feet (122 centimeters) in length and weigh as much as four people!

14. Scalefin anthias (*Pseudanthias squamipinnis*)
The sexes of these fish are quite different in color, the females being bright yellowy orange while the males are purple.

15. Bluestriped snapper (*Lutjanus kasmira*)
This nocturnal fish likes company, often swimming in shoals of up to 100 individuals looking for food around coral outcrops and shipwrecks.

16. Green sea turtle (*Chelonia mydas*)
Unlike most reptiles, the green turtle is entirely vegetarian, feeding mainly on seaweed. It might visit the Great Barrier Reef on one of its great migrations through the world's oceans. These remarkable marine creatures have been known to travel thousands of miles from their nesting beaches to feeding sites. They spend most of their life in the open sea, but the females of all turtle species come ashore to lay their eggs. Under cover of darkness, they dig a hole in the sandy beach above the tide mark and lay up to 100 eggs, carefully covering them with sand. The baby turtles will hatch some ten weeks later, scrambling in a dangerous journey back to the water. The females will return to the same beach years later to lay their own eggs.

17. Blue spot butterfly fish (*Chaetodon plebeus*)
The blue spot on its side and the black spot at the base of its tail are useful to this pretty butterflyfish – they confuse its enemies into thinking its tail is where its head should be.

18. Coral grouper (*Cephalopholis miniata*)
This colorful grouper reaches 16 inches (40 centimeters) and feeds on other fish.

19. Reticulated butterfly fish (*Chaetodon reticulatus*)
Like others of their kind, these fish look as if they have been squashed at the sides, resembling thin disks – an ideal shape for twisting and turning among the coral "forests" and hiding in narrow crevices.

20. Neon damsel (*Pomacentrus coelestris*)
Often found in plankton-feeding schools above the reef, the male of this species guards his nest of eggs, usually made among the rocks.

21. Trumpet fish (*Aulostomus chinensis*)
One of the pipefishes, this strange-looking fish can grow up to 16 inches (40 centimeters) in length.

22. Sharpnose puffer (*Canthigaster solandri*)
This stout little fish uses its tough teeth and jaws to eat sea urchins and marine crustaceans.

23. Fan worm (*Sabellastarte indica*)
With most of its body buried in sand, this fan worm relies on the fringe of its colorful crown to filter microscopic particles of food from the surrounding seawater. It will withdraw its fan into its body at the slightest sign of danger.

24. Brown star polyp (*Pachyclavularia violacea*)
Named for the color and shape of its tentacles, this coral often forms huge carpets on undersea ledges.

25. Pyjama cardinalfish (*Sphaeramia nematoplera*)
One of the most curiously marked reef fish, this species lives among branching coral.

26. Moon wrasse (*Thalassoma lunare*)
The brilliantly colored wrasse is highly territorial, only leaving its particular rocky patch to search for food.

27. Two-lined monocle bream (*Scolopsis bilneatus*)
When young, these fish hide among the coral, helped by their markings, which change as they grow.

28. Pink anemone fish (*Amphiprion perideraion*)
As its name suggests, this fish lives among the tentacles of certain types of sea anemone.

29. Bulb-tentacle anemone (*Entacmaea quadricolor*)
Easily identified by the fleshy lobes at the ends of its tentacles, this sea anemone feeds on small fish and other marine creatures.

Reef alert!

Some of the Earth's coral reefs have existed for many thousands of years, forming slowly as coral colonies build up on top of one another. Sadly, many reefs are being destroyed at a much faster rate than it takes them to grow. Natural events such as hurricanes can reduce reefs to rubble in minutes, while predators such as the infamous crown-of-thorns starfish eat away at the corals, leaving only the bony skeletons behind. But the greatest threat of all comes from humans...

Changes to the world's climate caused by global warming can cause the sea to heat up, and corals are sensitive to even the slightest change in temperature. If the water gets too warm, corals turn white (an effect known as "bleaching"), and although they may recover, very often the reef simply dies. Pollution too can poison the coral and its inhabitants, sewage and fertilizers can increase the growth of seaweeds and algae, which cover the coral in a suffocating carpet, and changes in land use often lead to reefs silting up or seawater becoming murky, cutting out the sunlight, which is vital for corals to grow.

Another problem is caused by irresponsible collectors, who roam the reefs taking corals, shells, fish, and other creatures to sell as souvenirs or for the aquarium trade. In some places coral is also mined from reefs and used to build houses or roads! Finally, tourism can have a bad effect because corals are easily damaged by trampling feet or anchoring boats, and polyps can easily be destroyed simply by being touched.

However, although tourism can damage reefs, it can also play a major role in saving them. Working together with wildlife agencies and conservation organizations, the tourist industry can assist in setting up marine parks where reefs are cared for and properly managed. It can help to educate people to understand the importance of reefs and care about their future, for not only are coral reefs vital for all the beautiful creatures that live there and for the people who depend on them for their livelihoods, but reefs also contain creatures that provide ingredients for drugs that may help cure human diseases such as cancer.

There are many organizations and agencies around the world dedicated to the conservation and protection of coral reefs. The Great Barrier Reef Marine Park is the largest marine park in the world, covering 138,000 square miles (357,000 square kilometers) of reefs and surrounding water. It helps manage the reef and plays a critical role in ensuring its survival while encouraging tourists. You can find out more about reefs and their conservation by contacting the organizations below.

World Wildlife Fund Australia runs a Great Barrier Reef Campaign. Learn about what you can do to help save reefs at *www.gbr.wwf.org.au*, or write to WWF Australia, GPO Box 528, Sydney, NSW 2001, Australia, or contact the World Wildlife Fund internationally at *www.panda.org* or by writing to World Wildlife Fund, PO Box 97180, Washington, DC 20090-7180, USA.

ReefBase is an international reef conservation project that features a large coral reef database. Find it at *www.reefbase.org*, or write to ReefBase Project, PO Box 500, GPO, 10670 Penang, Malaysia.

Part of the Australian Environmental Protection Agency, the **Queensland Parks and Wildlife Service** has a large section on the Great Barrier Reef. Find it at *www.env.qld.gov.au*, or write to Queensland Parks and Wildlife Service, PO Box 155, Albert Street, Brisbane QLD 4002, Australia.

The World Conservation Monitoring Centre site has a range of reef information. It can be contacted at *www.unep-wcmc.org*, or at its Information Office, UNEP-WCMC, 219 Huntingdon Road, Cambridge CB3 ODL, UK.

DISCARDED
Goshen Public Library

Pic
WAR

Ward, Helen,
Old shell, new
shell

OP

DISCARDED
Goshen Public Library